Instant Pot Cookbook

101 Quick, All Natural Instant Pot Recipes Under 30 Minutes With The Electric Pressure Cooker Cookbook

By

Kristen Carthredge

The information herein is offered for informational purposes solely, and is universal as so. The presentation of the information is without contract or any type of guarantee assurance.

The trademarks that are used are without any consent, and the publication of the trademark is without permission or backing by the trademark owner. All trademarks and brands within this book are for clarifying purposes only and are the owned by the owners themselves, not affiliated with this document.

Kristen Carthredge

Table of Contents

Introduction

I want to thank you and congratulate you for purchasing the book, *"Instant Pot Cookbook, 101 Quick, All Natural Instant Pot Recipes Under 30 Minutes With The Electric Pressure Cooker Cookbook."*

This book contains proven steps and strategies on how to use an Instant Pot to prepare simple yet delicious meals.

An Instant Pot is a simple device that cooks food in a shorter than normal time. Modeled after a traditional pressure cooker, it is meant to help cut down on 70% of the cooking time. But don't worry, this does not imply your food will taste any different or lack nutrition as the cooker ensures that both taste and nutrition are sealed within the ingredients.

The cooker is fairly easy to use and, with a little practice, just about anybody will be able to use it. It is a convenient device for busy people to use and keep them away from takeout and restaurant foods. This book will act as your electric cooker guide and teach you simple recipes that you can try out with yours.

The recipes are all tried and tested and sure to leave you wanting more. The book has been designed in such a way that you can easily navigate through the different chapters.

I hope you cook up a storm in the kitchen using your electric pressure cooker.

Thanks again for purchasing this book, I hope you enjoy it!

Chapter 1: Breakfast Recipes

Instant Pot Omelet

Ingredients:

- 5 eggs beaten
- 1/2 cup milk
- A pinch of salt
- Pepper to taste
- 5 bacon slices, cooked
- 1 cup sausage, cooked
- 1/2 cup ham, chopped
- 2 large onions, chopped
- 1 cup cheese, grated

Instructions:

- Add water to the bottom of the cooker. The water should rise to about 2 inches high.
- Add the eggs to a bowl along with the milk, salt and pepper and whisk until well combined.
- Add the chopped bacon to a bowl and crumbled sausages along with the ham and onions and mix until well combined.
- Add a spoonful of this into greased ramekins and press it down.
- Pour the eggy mixture over the top and shake the ramekins.
- Cover the ramekins using aluminum foil and use a strip to create a sling or handle. This will help you lift

up the dish with ease.

- Cook on high for 20 minutes and choose quick release.
- Now remove the ramekins out and allow the soufflé to cook through.
- You can serve with a sprinkling of parsley on top.

Breakfast Oats
Ingredients:

- 1 cup oats
- 3 cups water
- 1 teaspoon cinnamon powder
- 1 teaspoon nutmeg powder
- ¼ cup apples, chopped
- ¼ cup strawberries, chopped
- ¼ cup blueberries, chopped
- 1 tablespoons honey

Instructions:

- Add the oats to the Instant Pot along with the water and mix well.
- Tip in the cinnamon powder and nutmeg powder and mix well.
- Close the lid and choose manual 3 minutes.
- Once done, switch it off and allow the pressure to release naturally.
- Once done, check if the oats are watery, if so, then cover it again and allow the oats to absorb all of it.
- Once done, mix in the honey and combine.
- Serve the oats with a sprinkling of apples, strawberries, blueberries and any other fruits of your choice.

Cooker Quinoa
Ingredients:

- 2 cups quinoa
- Salt to taste
- Pepper to taste
- 3 cups chicken broth or water
- Juice of one lemon
- Mixed fresh herbs such as rosemary, thyme, chopped

Instructions:

- Add the quinoa to a bowl and rinse it thoroughly.
- Add water and lemon juice and mix well.
- Allow it to soak overnight.
- Next day, add the quinoa to the Instant Pot along with the salt and pepper and mix until well combined.
- Close the lid and cook the quinoa for 1 minute and switch off.
- Once done, switch it off and let the pressure release naturally.
- Add the rosemary and thyme and mix until combined.
- Serve hot.

Breakfast Bread
Ingredients:

- ½ cup butter, melted
- 1 cup plain sugar
- 2 large eggs, beaten
- 3 medium bananas, mashed
- 2 cups flour
- 2 teaspoons baking soda
- ½ teaspoon salt
- 1 cup almonds, chopped
- Chocolate chips to sprinkle
- Mint leaves to sprinkle

Instructions:

- Add the butter and sugar into a bowl and cream together.
- Add the eggs and beat until well combined.
- Add the bananas and mix until everything comes together.
- Tip in the flour, baking soda and salt and mix until well combined.
- Try to incorporate as little air as possible.
- Grease a cake pan with butter and flour or use cooking spray.
- You can also use a parchment paper at the bottom if you like.
- Pour water at the bottom of the cooker and place a trivet over it.
- Use an aluminum foil to create a sling and place it over the trivet such that the sides rise up.
- Place the cake pan over it.

- Cover and cook for 50 minutes on high.
- Allow the pressure to release naturally.
- Cool, cut and serve.

Cobbler

Ingredients:

- 1 pear, chopped
- 1 apple, chopped
- 1 plum, chopped
- 2 tablespoons honey
- 3 tablespoons coconut oil
- 1/2 teaspoon cinnamon powder
- 1/4 cup coconut, shredded
- 1/4 cup pecan nuts
- 2 tablespoons sunflower seeds

Instructions:

- Add the fruits to the cooker.
- Drizzle in the honey and coconut oil and mix well.
- Add the cinnamon and close the cooker.
- Pick manual for 10 minutes.
- Allow the steam to escape naturally or pick the natural release.
- Once done, remove the fruit out.
- Allow the juices to remain in the cooker.
- Tip in the coconut, pecans and sunflower seeds and mix well.
- Ensure you keep stirring it consistently so that you do not burn them.
- Once they are done, remove and mix them with the fruits.
- Serve hot.

Spicy Semolina

Ingredients:

- 2 cups semolina
- 4 cups water
- 1 carrot, chopped
- 1 cup French beans, chopped
- ½ cup peas
- 1 medium capsicum, chopped
- 1 large onion, chopped
- 1 tomato, chopped
- 3 chilies, chopped
- 1-inch ginger, minced
- 2 tablespoons vegetable oil
- 1 teaspoon mustard seeds
- 10 curry leaves
- Salt to taste
- Lemon juice to drizzle
- Cilantro to sprinkle

Instructions:

- Add the oil to the cooker and press the sauté button.
- Add the mustard seeds and allow them to splutter.
- Add the capsicum and curry leaves and mix.
- Tip in the chopped onions and sauté.
- Add the chilies and ginger and combine.
- Mix in the beans, carrot and peas and sauté for 5 minutes.
- Tip in the tomatoes and mix well.
- Add the semolina and mix until well combined.
- Add the water and mix well.
- Close and cook for 15 minutes.

- Allow the pressure to release naturally.
- Serve hot with a drizzle of lemon juice and fresh cilantro on top.

Instant Pot Rice Cakes
Ingredients:

- 1 cup split black lentil
- 4 cups special rice cake rice (idly rice)
- 2 cups thick beaten rice
- 1 tablespoon Fenugreek seeds
- 2 tablespoon Salt

Instructions:

- Add the lentils, rice, beaten rice and fenugreek seeds to separate bowls and add enough water to cover them.
- Allow it to stand for 3 to 6 hours.
- Add the seeds and beaten rice to a grinder along with a little water and grind until smooth.
- Add this to a bowl.
- Add the lentils and a little water and grind to a paste.
- Add this paste to the beaten rice mix and mix well.
- Add the rice to the grinder along with a little water and grind till smooth.
- Add this to the rest of the batter and mix well.
- Add the salt and use your hands to mix everything together in order to ferment the better.
- Cover and leave overnight.
- Next day, add enough water to the bottom of the cooker and place the trivet on top.
- Grease a rice cake stand with oil and pour a ladleful of the batter on top.
- Place it into the cooker and steam on high for 15 minutes.
- Choose the quick release option.
- Serve hot with mint chutney.

Instant Pot Vermicelli
Ingredients:

- 2 cups Vermicelli
- 2 cups water
- 5 Green chilies, slit
- Salt to taste
- 10-12 curry leaves
- 1 large onion, chopped
- 2 tablespoons vegetable oil
- 1 teaspoon mustard seeds
- 1 tablespoon lemon juice
- Cilantro to sprinkle

Instructions:

- Add the oil to the Instant Pot and pick the sauté option.
- Once it heats add the mustard seeds and allow it to sauté.
- Add the chilies and curry leaves and sauté.
- Tip in the onions and sauté until brown.
- Add the vermicelli and sauté for some time.
- Add the water and salt and mix until well combined.
- Add the lemon juice and mix well.
- Cover and cook for 10 minutes.
- Serve hot with a sprinkling of cilantro leaves on top.

Instant Pot Devilled Eggs
Ingredients:

- 10 eggs
- 1 cup water
- Paprika to taste
- 2 tablespoons mayonnaise
- 1 tablespoon olive oil
- 1 teaspoon mustard paste
- 1 teaspoon lemon juice
- Salt to taste
- Pepper to taste
- Cilantro to sprinkle

Instructions:

- Add the water to the Instant Pot and allow it to heat up before adding in the eggs.
- Cover and cook for 10 minutes or until the eggs are hard-boiled.
- Meanwhile, add the paprika, mayonnaise, oil, and mustard, lemon juice to a bowl and mix well.
- Once the eggs have cooled, halve it and use a spoon to scoop out the yolk.
- Add it to the bowl and mix well.
- Add this mixture into the centers of the egg whites.
- Sprinkle the salt and pepper on top and serve with a garnish of cilantro leaves.

Instant Pot Vegetable Breakfast Muffins

Ingredients:

- 5 eggs
- ¼ teaspoon pepper
- 4 tablespoons cheese
- 1 large onion, chopped
- 2 tablespoons French beans, chopped
- 2 tablespoons carrots, chopped
- ½ cup peas
- 2 tablespoon cauliflower, chopped
- 1 lemon, juiced
- Salt to taste
- Cilantro to sprinkle

Instructions:

- Add water to the cooker and place the steamer basket on top.
- Add the eggs to a bowl and mix in the pepper and whisk until well combined.
- Add the beans, carrots, peas, cauliflower, salt and lemon juice to a bowl and mix well.
- Add about 1 tablespoon of this mix into greased ramekins.
- Pour the eggy mixture over these vegetables and allow them to settle down.
- Place on the trivet and cover.
- Cook for 15 minutes.
- Serve hot with a sprinkling of cilantro leaves on top.

Chapter 2: Hearty Lunch Recipes

Chicken Biryani

Ingredients:

- 1 full chicken, chopped into bite size pieces
- 2 cups long grain or basmati rice
- 1 large onion, chopped
- 3 bay leaves
- 1/2-inch cinnamon stick
- 3 cardamom pods
- 5 cloves
- 1 teaspoon pepper
- 2-star anise
- 5 tablespoons ginger paste
- 5 tablespoons garlic paste
- 1/2 cup mint leaves, chopped
- 1/2 cup cilantro leaves, chopped
- 1 lemon, juiced and zested
- 5 green chilies, chopped
- 1 cup yogurt
- 3 tablespoons oil
- 3 tablespoons red chili powder
- 1 teaspoon turmeric powder
- 2 teaspoons cumin powder
- 2 tablespoons coriander powder
- 1 tablespoon curry powder
- Salt to taste
- Fried onions to sprinkle

Instructions:

- Add the yogurt to a bowl along with the lemon juice, curry powder, turmeric, chili powder, coriander powder and cumin powder and mix until well combined.
- Add 2 tablespoons of the ginger paste and 2 tablespoons of the garlic paste and mix until well combined.
- Toss the chicken into it and mix well.
- Add the salt and mix until well combined.
- Set it aside for 10 minutes.
- Add the oil to the pan and press sauté button.
- Add the onions to it and sauté till brown.
- Add the cardamom, cloves, cinnamon and bay leaves and mix well.
- Tip in the ginger, garlic paste and mix.
- Add the pepper and green chilies and mix well.
- Add the chicken to it and mix well.
- Tip in the rice and water and mix until well combined.
- Cover and cook for 20 minutes.
- Allow the steam to escape naturally.
- Once done, serve with a sprinkling of cilantro leaves and deep fried onions.

Seafood Paella
Ingredients:

- 1 pound shrimps
- 1-pound fish fillet
- 1 cup long grain rice
- ¼ cup butter
- ¼ cup parsley, chopped
- 1 teaspoon salt
- Pepper to taste
- Red pepper to taste
- 1 lemon, juiced
- 1 teaspoon saffron
- 2 cups chicken broth
- 4 cloves garlic, chopped
- Cilantro to sprinkle

Instructions:

- Add the shrimps and fish to the pressure cooker and arrange at the bottom.
- Pour in a little water and cook on high for 5 minutes.
- Use quick release.
- Now add the butter, rice, salt and pepper and mix.
- Sprinkle the red pepper and lemon juice and combine.
- Add the garlic on top.
- Add the saffron to the broth and mix until well combined.
- Add the broth to the cooker and combine.
- Close and cook on high for 20 minutes.
- Serve hot with a sprinkling of cilantro on top.

Whole Chicken
Ingredients:

- 1 medium onion, chopped
- 2 large carrots, chopped
- 3 celery stalks, chopped
- ½ garlic, chopped
- 3 cups water
- 1 whole chicken
- 2 bay leaves
- 1 tablespoon Thyme leaves
- 1 tablespoon oregano leaves
- Salt to taste
- Pepper to taste

Instructions:

- Add the garlic to the bottom of the Instant Pot followed by the carrots and celery and onions.
- Open the cavity of the chicken and stuff in the thyme and oregano leaves.
- Place the chicken over the vegetables and add the bay leaves on top.
- Sprinkle the salt and pepper over the chicken.
- Pour some water over it so that it reaches quarter way up to the chicken.
- Close the pot and choose the meat setting.
- Once done, pick manual 25 minutes.
- Allow the pressure to release naturally.
- This can take 15 to 20 minutes.
- Remember not to quick release as that can make the meat quite hard.
- Once done, remove your chicken out and place on a

plate.

- Use sharp knives to slice the chicken and serve hot with a drizzle of lemon juice.

Fish In Tomato Sauce

Ingredients:

- 1 large cod filet
- 1 cup tomatoes, chopped
- Salt to taste
- Pepper to taste
- 2 tablespoons butter
- Coriander leaves to sprinkle

Recipe:

- Add the butter to the Instant Pot and sauté for 2 minutes.
- Add the cod to a bowl along with the salt and pepper and rub well.
- Add the fish to the tomato and close the pot.
- Cook on manual for 10 minutes.
- Serve hot with a sprinkling of coriander leaves.

Pressure Cooker Chili

Ingredients:

- 1-pound beef, ground
- 2 teaspoons olive oil
- 1 large onion, chopped
- 1 bell pepper, chopped
- 1 jalapeno pepper, chopped
- 2 cloves garlic, chopped
- 2 cups kidney beans, drained and rinsed
- 2 cups tomatoes, chopped
- 3 tablespoons tomato paste
- 1 tablespoon brown sugar
- 2 teaspoons cocoa powder
- 1/4 teaspoon crushed red pepper flakes
- 2 tablespoons chili powder
- 2 teaspoons cumin powder
- Salt to taste
- Pepper to taste
- 2 cups water

Instructions:

- Add the beef to the cooker and sauté for 10 to 12 minutes or until brown.
- Remove to a plate and remove excess oil from it.
- Crumble it a little and set aside.
- Add the oil and fat from beef to the cooker.
- Mix in the onions, peppers and jalapenos and mix well.
- Add the garlic and sauté till brown.
- Mix in the kidney beans and tomatoes and sauté.
- Add the tomato paste, sugar, cocoa powder, red

pepper, chili powder, cumin powder and salt and mix well.

- Add the crumbled beef and water and mix well.
- Close the lid of the cooker and cook for 8 minutes.
- Allow the steam to escape naturally and serve hot.

Pork Roast
Ingredients:

- 2 pounds' pork meat
- 2 potatoes, chopped into chunks
- 10 to 12 button mushrooms, chopped
- 2 carrots, chopped
- 2 tablespoons cooking butter
- 2 tablespoons soya sauce
- 1 tablespoon olive oil
- 4 garlic cloves, chopped
- 2 bay leaves
- 1 tablespoon balsamic vinegar
- 1 cup chicken stock
- Salt to taste
- Pepper to taste
- 2 tablespoons corn flour
- 2 tablespoons water

Instructions:

- Add the oil to the cooker and pick the sauté option.
- Add the pork and wait for it to brown on all sides. You can flip it over every 5 minutes or so to ensure it is browned all around.
- Add the salt and pepper and rub it on the meat.
- Remove it from the pan.
- Toss in the garlic, mushrooms and add the butter with it.
- Allow them to brown a little.
- Add some salt and pepper to season it.
- The mushrooms should start releasing water; allow the water to evaporate while stirring continuously.

- Cut the pork into small pieces and add it to the cooker.
- Add the carrots and mix well.
- Add the bay leaves and mix until well combined.
- Add the vinegar to the cooker and scrape the bottom juices.
- Pour in the chicken stock and soya sauce and mix until well combined.
- Place the potatoes on top and close the cooker.
- Cook for 10 minutes on high and low for 5 minutes.
- Allow the steam to release naturally.
- Meanwhile, mix the cornstarch and water and make a thick paste.
- Add this to the cooker and mix.
- Sauté for 5 minutes or until it thickens.
- Remove the pork and slice it into thin slices.
- Serve hot with a drizzle of the sauce, vegetables and a sprinkling of cilantro leaves on top.

Kidney Bean Curry
Ingredients:

- 1 tablespoon olive oil
- 1 cup onion, chopped
- 2 cups bell pepper, chopped
- 2 teaspoons garlic, chopped
- 1 cup kidney beans
- 2 cups water
- 2 bay leaves
- 2 teaspoons dried thyme
- 2 teaspoons smoked paprika
- 2 teaspoons dried marjoram
- 1/2 teaspoon cayenne pepper powder
- 1 tablespoon lemon juice
- Fresh cream
- Cilantro to sprinkle

Instructions:

- Press the sauté feature of the Instant Pot and add the oil.
- Add the onions and brown them on all sides.
- Toss in the garlic and pepper and mix well.
- Tip in the thyme, bay leaves, paprika, marjoram and cayenne powder and mix until well combined.
- Add the kidney beans and water and mix well.
- Add the lemon juice and cover the cooker.
- Cook for 15 minutes.
- Allow the pressure to release naturally.
- Once done, remove the bay leaves and discard them.
- Serve with a drizzle of cream and a sprinkling of fresh cilantro on top.

Meatballs With Pasta
Ingredients:

- 1-pound ground beef
- 1 tablespoon basil leaves
- 1 teaspoon marjoram leaves
- 1/2 teaspoon thyme leaves
- 2 tablespoons olive oil
- 1 large fennel, chopped
- 1 large onion, chopped
- 1 medium bell pepper, membrane and seeds removes, chopped
- 1 cup pasta of your choice
- 3 cups tomatoes, chopped
- 1 cup chicken broth
- 1/2 cup dry white wine
- 1 tablespoon oregano
- 1/2 teaspoon rosemary
- 1/2 teaspoon nutmeg
- Salt to taste
- Pepper to taste
- Cilantro to sprinkle

Instructions:

- Add the beef to a bowl along with the basil, marjoram and thyme and mix until well combined.
- Add the oil to the cooker and toss in the onion and fennel.
- Brown a little.
- Meanwhile, make small meatballs out of the mixture and set aside.
- Add the bell peppers to the cooker and sauté them.

- Add the pasta and tomatoes and mix well.
- Tip in the wine, oregano, rosemary, and nutmeg and mix until well combined.
- Add the salt and broth and mix.
- Add the meatballs on top of it and close the cooker.
- Cook on high for 5 to 10 minutes.
- Use the quick release option to release the steam.
- Serve hot with a sprinkling of fresh cilantro on top.

Pulled Steak
Ingredients:

- 3 cups water
- 2 pounds' steak
- 2 bay leaves
- Salt to taste
- 5 tablespoons vegetable oil
- 1 large onion, chopped
- 1 green bell pepper, chopped
- 1 red bell pepper, chopped
- 4 garlic, chopped
- 1 teaspoon oregano leaf
- 1/2 teaspoon cumin powder
- 1 cup tomato sauce
- 1 cup red wine
- 1 tablespoon vinegar
- Pepper to taste
- Cilantro to sprinkle

Instructions:

- Add the steak to the cooker along with the bay leaves and water.
- Tip in the salt and mix well.
- Cover and cook on high for 15 minutes.
- Lower it and cook for another 15 minutes.
- Once done, remove the steak out.
- Add the oil to the cooker and toss in the onions to sauté.
- Meanwhile, shred the pork using a fork or do so with just your hands.
- Add the garlic and mix well.

- Toss in the bell peppers along with the cumin and oregano and mix well.
- Sauté until they release their aroma.
- Add the tomatoes along with the red wine and beef stock and mix well.
- Add the salt and pepper and mix well.
- Add the pulled meat and mix.
- Cook on high for 10 minutes.
- Serve hot with a sprinkling of cilantro leaves on top.

Mac And Cheese
Ingredients:

- 3 cups chicken broth
- 1-pound macaroni pasta
- 2 cups water
- 8 ounces whipping cream
- 1 cup Cheddar cheese, grated
- 1 cup mozzarella cheese, grated
- 8 ounces' cream cheese
- 3 tablespoons butter
- 1 tablespoon Parmesan cheese, grated
- 1 teaspoon mustard paste
- 1 tablespoon oregano leaves
- ½ teaspoon thyme leaves
- ½ teaspoon rosemary leaves
- Salt to taste
- Pepper to taste
- Parsley to sprinkle

Instructions:

- Add the chicken broth to the cooker along with the macaroni and mix well.
- Add the cheddar and mozzarella cheese and mix well.
- Add the mustard and salt and combine.
- Toss in the thyme, oregano and rosemary and mix.
- Add the Parmesan cheese and mix.
- Close the cooker and cook for 20 minutes.
- Allow the steam to escape naturally.
- Serve hot with a sprinkling of parsley leaves on top.

Anchovy Chili

Ingredients:

- 3 pounds' beef ribs, with bone
- Salt to taste
- Pepper to taste
- 1 teaspoon cumin powder
- 1 tablespoon chili powder
- 2 tablespoons olive oil
- 2 tablespoons garlic, chopped
- ½ cup cilantro leaves, chopped
- 1 teaspoon jalapeño pepper, chopped
- 2 cups beef broth
- 1/4 cup brown sugar
- 1 cup wine, preferably red

Instructions:

- Clean the ribs and pat them down.
- Add the salt and pepper and season them well.
- Add the cumin and chili and rub it in.
- Add the oil to the cooker and allow it to heat up.
- Add the ribs and brown them on all sides. Flip them every 5 minutes once.
- Remove it out.
- Add the garlic and onions and sauté till brown.
- Add the jalapeno and sugar and pepper and mix.
- Sauté for a minute and add to a blender along with the broth, cilantro and whizz until smooth.
- Add this back to the cooker along with the wine and mix.
- Add the ribs back and cover.
- Cook on high for 25 minutes.

- Allow the steam to escape naturally, can take 10 to 15 minutes.
- Once done, remove the ribs out and carve.
- Serve with the sauce on top.

Chickpea Stew
Ingredients:

- 2 cups spinach leaves
- 5 tablespoons olive oil
- 2 garlic cloves, chopped
- 1 tablespoon pine nuts
- Salt to taste
- Pepper to taste
- 1 cup water
- 1 cup chickpeas
- 1 large onion, chopped
- 2 carrots, chopped
- 1 cup tomatoes, chopped
- 4 cups water
- Parsley to sprinkle

Instructions:

- Soak the chickpeas in water overnight in order to help them swell up.
- Add the oil to the cooker and press the sauté button.
- Add the onion and garlic and sauté for 3 minutes.
- Once it browns, toss in the pine nuts and brown them.
- Add the carrots and tomatoes and mix well.
- Add the chickpeas and water and mix.
- Add the spinach and well combine.
- Cover and cook on high for 15 minutes.
- Allow the pressure to release naturally.
- Serve hot with a sprinkling of parsley leaves on top.

Chinese Ribs
Ingredients:

- 3 tablespoons paprika powder
- 1 tablespoon garlic, chopped
- Salt to taste
- Pepper to taste
- 6 pounds' pork ribs
- 2 tablespoons vegetable oil
- 3 cups water
- 1/2 cup ketchup
- 5 tablespoons brown sugar
- 2 tablespoons lemon juice

Instructions:

- Add the paprika, garlic, salt and pepper to a bowl and toss in the ribs.
- Rub it into the ribs so as to coat it thoroughly. Set it aside.
- Add the oil to the cooker and allow it to heat up.
- Add the ribs to it and roast on all sides.
- Turn after 5 minutes on each side.
- Add the water, ketchup, sugar, and vinegar to a bowl and mix well.
- Add this to the ribs and mix until well combined.
- Cover and cook on medium for 20 minutes.
- Release the pressure naturally.
- Serve hot.

Coconut Chicken
Ingredients:

- 1 tablespoon olive oil
- 1 onion, chopped
- 1 ½ inch ginger, chopped
- 3 garlic cloves, chopped
- 1 tablespoon curry powder
- 1 teaspoon turmeric powder
- 2 pounds' chicken thighs
- Salt to taste
- Pepper to taste
- 1 cup coconut milk
- 1/2 cup water
- 2 cups rice, cleaned
- 2 tablespoons cilantro leaves
- 2 teaspoons sugar
- 1 lemon, juiced
- Parsley leaves to sprinkle

Instructions:

- Press the sauté button of the cooker.
- Add the oil followed by the onions and garlic and sauté until brown.
- Add the turmeric and curry powder and mix well.
- Toss in the chicken and sprinkle the salt and pepper on top.
- Add the coconut milk and combine.
- Cook on manual for 15 minutes.
- Pick the quick release option to release the steam from the cooker.
- Add the rice, cilantro leaves and sugar and mix well.

- Cover and cook on manual for 15 minutes.
- Once done, squeeze the lemon and mix well.
- Serve hot with a sprinkling of parsley leaves on top.

Greek Beef Stew

Ingredients:

- 1 tablespoon olive oil
- 1-pound beef meat, minced
- 1 large onion, chopped
- 1 large garlic, chopped
- 1/4 cup red wine
- 2 tablespoons vinegar
- 1/2 cup chicken broth
- 1 tablespoon tomato puree
- 1/2 teaspoon rosemary
- 1/2 teaspoon oregano
- 5 black peppercorns
- 2 bay leaves
- 1 teaspoon cumin powder
- 1/4 teaspoon cinnamon powder
- ¼ teaspoon clove powder
- 2 tablespoons sugar
- 1 cup tomatoes
- 1/2 cup water
- 2 potatoes, chopped
- 2 carrots, chopped
- Salt to taste
- Cilantro to sprinkle

Instructions:

- Add the oil to the cooker and allow it to heat up.
- Add the beef and mix well.
- Take it out on a plate.
- Add the onions and sauté till brown.
- Add the garlic and brown.

- Add the potatoes and carrots and mix well.
- Add the tomato puree and vinegar and mix.
- Add the chicken stock and mix until well combined.
- Add the rosemary and oregano and mix well.
- Add the black peppers and mix.
- Add the bay leaves and cumin along with the cinnamon, cloves and sugar and mix well.
- Add the water and mix well.
- Close the cooker and cook on manual for 20 minutes.
- Serve hot with a sprinkling of cilantro leaves on top.

Beer Turkey
Ingredients:

- 1 tablespoon oil
- 2 teaspoons coriander powder
- 1 teaspoon mustard paste
- Salt to taste
- Pepper to taste
- 1/2 teaspoon garlic, minced
- 2 turkey thighs, slit
- 1 bottle beer dark beer
- 2 tablespoons brown sugar
- 2 tablespoons lemon juice
- 2 tomatoes, chopped
- Cilantro to sprinkle

Instructions:

- Add the coriander, mustard, salt and pepper to a bowl and mix well.
- Add the turkey thighs and coat it with this mixture.
- Add the beer to the cooker and place the chicken in between.
- Close the cooker and cook on high for 15 minutes.
- Allow the steam to escape naturally or press the quick release button to release the steam out.
- Remove the gravy and turkey and cut it into small pieces.
- Add the oil to the pan and toss in the garlic.
- Add the tomatoes and sauté.
- Return the sauce to it along with the turkey and mix well.
- Add the lemon juice and mix.

- Cook for 5 minutes.
- Serve hot with a sprinkling of cilantro leaves on top.

Sweet Potato Curry

Ingredients:

- 2 large sweet potatoes, chopped
- Salt to taste
- 2 tablespoons brown sugar
- 1/2 teaspoon cinnamon powder
- 1/4 teaspoon nutmeg powder
- 1 cup water
- 2 tablespoons butter

Instructions:

- Peel the sweet potatoes and cut them into halves.
- Chop them into smaller pieces.
- Add them to the cooker.
- Season them with the salt.
- Add the sugar, cinnamon and nutmeg to a bowl and mix well.
- Sprinkle this over the sweet potatoes.
- Add the water and mix well.
- Add the butter on top of it and close the cooker.
- Cook on high for 20 minutes.
- Once done, check if all the water is evaporated.
- If not, sauté for 2-3 minutes.
- Serve hot.

Indian Style Sticky Rice
Ingredients:

- 5 tablespoons vegetable oil
- 10 to 12 cashew nuts
- 2 chili peppers
- 1 teaspoon cumin seeds
- 1 teaspoon mustard seeds
- 10 black peppercorns
- 1 pinch asafoetida powder
- 10 to 12 curry leaves
- 1 cup split yellow lentils
- 1 cup rice
- 2 green chili peppers, chopped
- 1/2 teaspoon turmeric powder
- Salt to taste
- 4 cups water
- 2 tablespoons clarified butter
- Cilantro to sprinkle
- Coconut shreds to sprinkle

Instructions:

- Add the oil to the cooker and press sauté.
- Add the cashews and brown them.
- Remove them on a plate.
- Toss in the mustard, asafoetida, and green chili and curry leaves and brown them.
- Add the cumin seeds and red chilies and brown.
- Add the peppercorns and salt and mix well.
- Toss in the rice and lentils and mix.
- Add the water and mix well.
- Cover the cooker and cook on high for 15 minutes.

- Once done, add the clarified butter on top and mix well.
- Serve hot with a sprinkling of cilantro and coconut on top.

Black-Eyed Peas Curry With Spinach
Ingredients:

- 1 large onion, chopped
- 3 garlic, chopped
- 1 cup red pepper, chopped
- 1 small jalapeño, chopped
- 2 teaspoons paprika
- 2 teaspoons chili powder
- 2 cups black eyed peas
- 4 dates, chopped
- 2 cups vegetable broth
- 1 cup tomatoes, chopped
- 2 green chilies, chopped
- 2 cups mixed greens
- Salt to taste
- Pepper to taste
- Parsley to sprinkle

Instructions:

- Press sauté on the Instant Pot and add the oil.
- Toss in the onions and garlic and sauté for 2 minutes or until brown.
- Add the peppers and sauté for a few minutes.
- Add the chili powder, paprika and mix well.
- Add the black-eyed peas and mix well.
- Add the water and cover the cooker.
- Cook on high for 15 minutes.
- Once open, add the greens, tomatoes and mix well.
- Cover and cook for a further 1 minutes.
- Add the salt and pepper and sauté until the sauce reduces a little.
- Add the parsley on top and serve.

Vegetable Pilaf
Ingredients:

- 2 cups basmati or long grain rice
- 3 tablespoons clarified butter
- 1 large onion, chopped
- 1/2 teaspoon cumin seeds
- 2 bay leaves, halved
- 2 potatoes, chopped
- 2 carrots, chopped
- 2 teaspoons turmeric powder
- 1 teaspoon chili powder
- 1 teaspoon coriander powder
- 2 1/2 cups water
- 1 cup peas
- Salt to taste
- Pepper to taste
- 1 teaspoon butter
- 1/2 teaspoon curry powder

Instructions:

- Add the rice to a bowl along with the water and allow it to soak for 20 minutes.
- Drain the water away.
- Add the oil to the cooker and let it heat up.
- Toss in the onion, cumin and bay leaves and allow them to release their flavor into the oil.
- Add the potatoes and carrots and mix well.
- Mix in the turmeric, chili powder and coriander and mix until well combined.
- Add the rice and mix in gently.
- Toss in the peas and butter and mix well.

- Add the curry powder and water and mix.
- Cover and cook on high for 15 minutes or until the rice is all fluffy.
- Serve hot with a sprinkling of fresh cilantro on top.

Chicken Enchiladas
Ingredients:

- 1-pound chicken thighs, trimmed
- 2 cups chili sauce
- 1/2 cup onion, chopped
- 12 corn tortillas
- 3 tablespoons vegetable oil
- 1/2 cup mozzarella cheese
- 1 tablespoon parmesan cheese
- Cilantro to sprinkle

Instructions:

- Add the chicken thighs to the Instant Pot along with the chili sauce and mix.
- Close the lid and cook on high for 10 minutes and then quick release.
- Remove the chicken to a bowl.
- Once it cools, pull it using forks.
- Add chili sauce to the bowl and ensure the chicken is completely coated.
- Add the onion to a bowl and along with the cheeses and mix.
- Add the trivet to the cooker and brush the tortillas with oil.
- Place the tortillas on the trivet and broil for 5 minutes.
- Once done, remove and place on a plate.
- Add about a tablespoon of the chili in the center and sprinkle the onion, cheese mix over it.
- Roll it up slightly and keep it folded.
- Serve with a sprinkling of cilantro on top.

Chapter 3: Dinner Recipes

Beef and vegetable stew
Ingredients:

- 3 tablespoons vegetable oil
- 1/4 cup flour
- 1/2 teaspoon paprika powder
- Salt to taste
- Pepper to taste
- 1/4 teaspoon cumin powder
- 1/4 teaspoon oregano
- 1/4 teaspoon garlic, chopped
- 2 pounds' beef, chopped
- 2 garlic, chopped
- 2 cups tomatoes, chopped
- 2 cups beef broth
- 2 bay leaves
- 1/2 teaspoon red pepper flakes
- 3 large potatoes, chopped
- 2 large carrots, chopped
- 2 cups corn
- 1/2 onion, chopped
- 1/2 cabbage, chopped
- Parsley leaves to sprinkle

Instructions:

- Set the cooker on sauté.
- Add the oil and allow it to heat up.

- Add the flour, paprika, salt, pepper, cumin, oregano and garlic to a bowl and mix until well combined.
- Add the beef and coat it thoroughly.
- Add it to the cooker and brown it on all sides.
- Remove it out.
- Add oil to the cooker.
- Add the garlic to the cooker and allow it to sauté.
- Add the tomatoes and mix well.
- Add the broth and mix well.
- Toss in the bay leaves, pepper and potatoes and mix well.
- Tip in the carrots and corn and mix well.
- Add the onions and cabbage and mix well.
- Close the cooker and cook on manual for 20 minutes.
- Serve hot with a sprinkling of cilantro leaves on top.

Creamy Pork
Ingredients:

- 1-pound pork meat, chopped
- 3 tablespoons corn flour
- Salt to taste
- Pepper to taste
- 2 tablespoons olive oil
- 1 cup white wine
- 2 carrots, chopped
- 1 celery, chopped
- 6 prunes, chopped
- Cilantro to sprinkle

Instructions:

- Tenderize the meat by beating it down.
- Add the cornstarch to a bowl along with the salt and pepper and mix well.
- Add the meat and coat thoroughly.
- Add the oil to the cooker and allow it to heat up.
- Toss in the meat and brown it on all sides.
- Add the wine, carrots, celery and prunes and mix well.
- Cook on manual for 20 minutes.
- Serve hot with a sprinkling of cilantro leaves on top.

Lamb With Beans
Ingredients:

- 1 cup cannellini beans
- 2 lamb shanks
- Salt to taste
- Pepper to taste
- 2 tablespoons flour
- 2 tablespoons olive oil
- 2 shallots, chopped
- 2 carrots, chopped
- 2 celery ribs, chopped
- 5 cloves garlic, chopped
- 2 teaspoons fresh rosemary, chopped
- 1 cup red wine
- 2 cups beef broth
- 1 cup water
- 1 tablespoon tomato paste
- 2 teaspoons lemon zest
- Parsley to sprinkle

Instructions:

- Add the lamb to a bowl along with the salt and pepper and rub it in.
- Add the oil to the cooker and allow it to heat up.
- Add the lamb and brown on all sides.
- Toss in the shallots and brown them.
- Tip in the carrots, celery, rosemary, and wine and beef broth and mix well.
- Add the water and tomato paste and mix until well combined.
- Add the wine, lemon zest and mix well.

- Cover and cook on manual for 20 minutes.
- Serve warm with a sprinkling of fresh parsley leaves on top.

Instant Pot Beef And Vegetables
Ingredients:

- 2 tablespoons vegetable oil
- 3 pounds' beef roast, chopped
- Salt to taste
- Pepper to taste
- 1 large onion, chopped
- 1 cup beef broth
- 2 teaspoons Worcestershire sauce
- 4 carrots, chopped
- 4 potatoes, chopped
- Parsley leaves to sprinkle

Instructions:

- Add the oil to the cooker and allow it to heat up.
- Add the onions and sauté them.
- Add the beef roast and mix well.
- Add the carrots and potatoes and mix well.
- Toss in the broth and mix well.
- Add the salt and pepper and combine.
- Cover and cook on manual for 15 minutes.
- Serve warm with a sprinkling of fresh parsley leaves on top.

Instant Pot Sausage Pasta
Ingredients:

- 1 tablespoon olive oil
- ½ cup bacon, chopped
- 1 cup sausage meat, chopped
- 1 onion, chopped
- 2 garlic, chopped
- 2 cups tomato puree
- Salt to taste
- Pepper to taste
- 1 cup pasta
- 1 cup water
- 2 tablespoons basil leaves
- Cilantro to sprinkle

Instructions:

- Add the oil to the cooker and warm it.
- Add the onion and garlic and brown it.
- Toss in the bacon and sauté.
- Add the sausage meat and mix.
- Add the tomato puree along with salt and pepper and mix until well combined.
- Add the pasta, water and basil leaves and mix well.
- Cover and cook on manual for 25 minutes.
- Serve warm with a sprinkling of fresh cilantro leaves on top.

Instant Pot Tangy Potatoes
Ingredients:

- 2 pounds' potatoes
- 1/2 cup water
- 1/2 tablespoon butter
- 1/2 cup milk
- 1/2 cup Greek yogurt
- 1/2 teaspoon garlic, chopped
- Salt to taste
- Pepper to taste
- Cilantro to sprinkle

Instructions:

- Add the butter to the cooker and heat it up.
- Toss in the potatoes and brown them.
- Add the garlic and sauté.
- Add the yogurt and mix until well combined.
- Add the water and mix well.
- Cover the cooker and cook on manual for 15 minutes.
- Serve warm with a sprinkling of fresh cilantro leaves on top.

Glazed Meatballs
Ingredients:

- 1-pound beef mince
- 2/3 cup breadcrumbs
- 1 egg white
- 1 onion, chopped
- 5 Garlic cloves, chopped
- 5 olives, chopped
- 2 fresh basil leaves, chopped
- Salt to taste
- Pepper to taste
- 1 Tablespoon brown sugar
- 1 Tablespoon mustard
- 1/4 cup ketchup
- Cilantro to sprinkle

Instructions:

- Add the oil to the cooker and toss in the onion and garlic.
- Sauté till brown.
- Add it to a bowl and mix in the meat.
- Add the olive basil, salt and pepper and make small balls out of it.
- Add the ketchup, brown sugar and mustard to the cooker and mix until well combined.
- Add the balls to it one by one and cover the cooker.
- Cook on manual for 20 minutes.
- Serve warm with a sprinkling of fresh cilantro leaves on top.

Chile Verde
Ingredients:

- 3 pounds' chicken thighs
- 3 pounds' tomato
- 1-pound bell peppers, chopped
- 2 jalapeño chilies, chopped
- 2 onions, chopped
- 5 garlic cloves, chopped
- 1 tablespoon cumin seeds
- 1 tablespoon oil
- Salt to taste
- Pepper to taste
- 1 cup chicken stock
- Cilantro to sprinkle
- Tortillas and lemon to serve

Instructions:

- Add the oil to the cooker and toss in the onions to brown.
- Add the garlic and sauté.
- Toss in the cumin, salt and pepper and mix well.
- Add the jalapenos, bell peppers and chicken things and sauté them.
- Add the salt and pepper and mix well.
- Add the tomatoes and stock and mix well.
- Cover the cooker and cook on manual for 20 minutes.
- Sprinkle the cilantro on top.
- Serve by placing it in the tortillas and squeezing the lemon on top.

Pork Caritas

Ingredients:

- 1 tablespoon chili powder
- 2 teaspoons paprika powder
- 2 teaspoons cumin powder
- 1 teaspoon coriander powder
- ½ teaspoon dried oregano
- Salt to taste
- Pepper to taste
- 4 pounds' pork shoulder
- 2 tablespoons coconut oil
- 1 bottle beer
- 2 oranges, juiced and zested
- 1 onion, chopped
- 3 garlic cloves, chopped
- 2 bay leaves
- Cilantro to sprinkle

Instructions:

- Add the oil to the cooker and toss in the pork shoulder.
- Brown it on all sides.
- Toss in the onions and brown them.
- Toss in the cumin, paprika, chili powder, coriander powder, salt and pepper and mix until well combined.
- Add the oregano, beer and orange juice and mix until well combined.
- Add the bay leaves and close the cooker.
- Cook on manual for 20 minutes.
- Serve warm with a sprinkling of fresh cilantro leaves on top.

Chicken Risotto
Ingredients:

- 1 onion, chopped
- 2 garlic cloves, chopped
- 5 tablespoons butter
- 1 tablespoon olive oil
- Salt to taste
- Pepper to taste
- 1-pound chicken breasts, chopped
- 1 cup Arborio rice
- 4 tablespoons parmesan
- 100 ml wine
- 2 cups chicken stock
- 1 tablespoon thyme leaves
- 1 tablespoon rosemary leaves
- Parsley to sprinkle

Instructions:

- Add the oil to the cooker and toss in the onions.
- Allow them to brown before adding in the garlic and browning them.
- Add the chicken and brown it.
- Add the rice and mix it in well.
- Add the thyme and rosemary and mix until well combined.
- Add the butter and mix well.
- Now add the chicken stock batch by batch.
- You must wait for it to be fully absorbed before adding in some more stock.
- Once done, add the wine and mix well.
- Gently stir in the cheese and mix well.

- Cover the cooker and cook on manual for 15 minutes.
- Serve warm with a sprinkling of fresh parsley leaves on top.

Beef Rouladen

Ingredients:

- 2 pounds' beef ribs
- 1 large onion, chopped
- ½ celery, chopped
- ½ cup prunes
- 2 garlic cloves, chopped
- ¼ cup butter
- Salt to taste
- Pepper to taste
- 1 tablespoon tomato puree
- 4 carrots, chopped
- 1 cup of beef stock
- 2 bay leaves
- 1 teaspoon thyme
- 1 teaspoon rosemary
- Parsley to sprinkle

Instructions:

- Add the butter to the cooker and allow it to heat up before adding in the onions and sauté till brown.
- Add the celery and brown.
- Toss in the garlic along with the salt and pepper and brown.
- Tip in the carrots and bay leaves and mix well.
- Add the tomato and mix until well combined.
- Toss in the thyme, rosemary and mix well.
- Add the beef stock and mix until well combined.
- Toss in the beef and cover the cooker.
- Cook on manual for 25 minutes.
- Serve warm with a sprinkling of fresh parsley leaves on top.

Chicken Romano
Ingredients:

- 1 cup flour
- Salt to taste
- Pepper to taste
- 5 chicken breasts, chopped
- 2 tablespoons oil
- 1 onion, chopped
- 1 cup tomato puree
- 1 teaspoon lemon juice
- 1 cup mushrooms, chopped
- 1 tablespoon sugar
- 1 teaspoon garlic, chopped
- 1 tablespoon oregano leaves
- 1 teaspoon basil leave
- 1 cup parmesan cheese

Instructions:

- Add the oil to the cooker and allow it to heat up.
- Toss in the onion and garlic and allow them to brown.
- Add the chicken and brown it all around.
- Tip in the mushrooms and mix well.
- Add the lemon juice and sugar and mix until well combined.
- Add the tomato puree along with the oregano and basil and mix until well combined.
- Add the flour and cover the cooker.
- Cook on manual for 10 minutes.
- Add the cheese.
- Cook for further 5 minutes.
- Serve hot.

Instant Pot Lasagna
Ingredients:

- 1 pack lasagna noodles
- 1 cup pasta sauce
- 1 cup Ricotta cheese
- 5 tablespoons parmesan cheese, grated
- 1 cup Italian sausage, chopped
- 1 cup fresh mushrooms, chopped
- Salt to taste
- Pepper to taste
- Cilantro leaves to sprinkle

Instructions:

- Add the oil to a spring form pan.
- Break up the noodles and add to the pan.
- Add the cheese on top of it and spread using a fork.
- Break up the sausages and add it on top of the cheese.
- Add the mushrooms on top.
- Repeat these layers as many times as you like.
- Sprinkle the salt and pepper over the last layer on top.
- Add water to the bottom of the cooker and place the trivet in it.
- Add the pan over it and cover it with foil.
- Cook on manual for 15 minutes.
- Serve hot with a sprinkling of cilantro leaves on top.

Honey Lemon Chicken Wings
Ingredients:

- 2 pounds' chicken wings
- 4 garlic cloves, chopped
- 1 large onion, chopped
- 2 whole star anise
- 1 tablespoon ginger, chopped
- 1 tablespoon honey
- ½ cup lemon juice
- 1 cup warm water
- 1 tablespoon olive oil
- 2 tablespoon cornstarch
- 2 tablespoons soya sauce
- 1 teaspoon sugar
- Salt to taste
- Pepper to taste
- Parsley to sprinkle

Instructions:

- Add the ginger, honey, lemon juice, soya sauce, sugar, salt and pepper to a bowl and mix until well combined.
- Add the chicken wings and mix well.
- Allow it to stand for 30 minutes to an hour.
- Place the cooker on sauté mode and add the oil.
- Toss in the garlic and brown it.
- Add the star anise and mix well.
- Add the water and mix well.
- Add the marinated chicken and mix well.
- Cover and cook on manual for 20 minutes.
- Serve hot with a sprinkling of parsley on top.

Lamb Curry
Ingredients:

- 2 pounds' lamb shoulder, chopped
- 10 garlic cloves, chopped
- 2 onions, chopped
- 1 tablespoon ginger, chopped
- 1 large potato, chopped
- 1 tablespoon cilantro, chopped
- 2 tablespoons olive oil
- 3 tablespoons curry powder
- ¼ teaspoon chili powder
- ½ cup tomato puree
- 2 cups water
- Salt to taste
- Pepper to taste
- Cilantro to sprinkle

Instructions:

- Heat the cooker and set it on sauté.
- Add the oil and allow it to warm up.
- Add the lamb and roast it on all sides.
- Toss in the salt and pepper and mix well.
- Remove it out.
- Toss in the onion, ginger and garlic and mix until well combined.
- Sauté it for 2 minutes or until brown.
- Add the curry powder and mix until well combined.
- Tip in the chili powder along with the water and mix.
- Add the potatoes and tomato puree and combine.
- Add the cilantro leaves and cover the cooker.
- Cook on manual for 20 minutes.
- Allow the steam to escape naturally.
- Serve hot with a sprinkling of cilantro on top.

Mango Lentil Curry
Ingredients:

- 1 tablespoon coconut oil
- 1 teaspoon cumin seeds
- 1 large onion, chopped
- 4 garlic, chopped
- 1 tablespoon fresh ginger, chopped
- 1 teaspoon coriander powder
- 1/8 teaspoon cayenne pepper powder
- Salt to taste
- 1 cup yellow lentil
- 4 cups water
- 1 teaspoon turmeric powder
- 2 mangos, chopped
- 1 lemon, juiced and zested
- Cilantro to sprinkle

Instructions:

- Add the lentils to a bowl and rinse until clean.
- Press sauté on the cooker and toss in the oil and cumin.
- Once it splutters, add the onions and brown them.
- Add the garlic, ginger and coriander and brown them.
- Toss in the cayenne and salt and mix well.
- Add the lentils and mangoes to the cooker and mix well.
- Add the water and lemon juice and mix well until combined.
- Cover and cook on manual for 15 minutes.
- Serve hot with a sprinkling of cilantro on top.

Indian Kadhi
Ingredients:

- ½ cup gram flour
- 1 cup yogurt
- 6 cups water
- Salt to taste
- 1 teaspoon turmeric powder
- 1/2 teaspoon fenugreek seeds
- ½ teaspoon mustard seeds
- 1 teaspoon carom seeds
- 10 curry leaves
- 4 dry red chilies
- 2 green chilies, slit
- Parsley leaves to sprinkle

Instructions:

- Add the flour to a bowl along with the yogurt and water and mix until well combined.
- Add the turmeric and salt and mix well.
- Set the cooker on sauté and add the oil.
- Toss in the fenugreek and mustard seeds along with the carom seeds and wait for them to splutter.
- Add the curry leaves and brown them.
- Tip in the red chilies and mix.
- Now pour in the yogurt mix and mix until well combined.
- Cover and cook on high for 20 minutes.
- Serve hot with a sprinkling of parsley leaves on top.

Balsamic Chicken
Ingredients:

- 1-pound chicken thighs
- 2 tablespoons parsley, chopped
- 1 teaspoon garlic, chopped
- 1 teaspoon basil, chopped
- Salt to taste
- Pepper to taste
- 1 green onion, chopped
- 2 tablespoons olive oil
- 2 tablespoons balsamic vinegar
- 1 teaspoon Worcestershire sauce
- 1/3 cup wine
- Parsley to sprinkle

Instructions:

- Add the basil, salt, pepper, wine and sherry to a bowl and mix until well combined.
- Add the chicken to it and mix well. Coat it thoroughly.
- Allow it to sit for 2 to 6 hours.
- Set the cooker on sauté and add the oil.
- Toss in the garlic and sauté until brown.
- Add the chicken and mix.
- Add the vinegar and sauce and mix well.
- Cover and cook for 15 minutes.
- All the pressure to escape naturally.
- Serve hot with a sprinkling of parsley leaves on top.

Coconut Sweet Rice
Ingredients:

- 1 cup short grain rice
- 2 cups water
- 1 cup coconut milk
- Pinch of salt
- ¼ cup brown sugar
- 1/2 cup milk
- 1 teaspoon vanilla
- 1 mango, chopped
- Roasted Almonds to garnish
- Coconut to garnish

Instructions:

- Add the water to the cooker and bring to the bowl.
- Add the rice and salt and mix until well combined.
- Add the milk and vanilla and mix.
- Toss in the sugar and mix until well combined.
- Cover and cook on manual for 20 minutes.
- Allow the steam to escape.
- If there is still excess water, then place on sauté to soak it up.
- Serve hot with a sprinkling of mango on top.

Braised Turkey Thighs
Ingredients:

- 2 turkey thighs, trimmed
- 1 cup chicken broth
- 1 lemon, juiced and zested
- 1 cup onion, chopped
- 1 cup mushrooms, chopped
- 2 teaspoons garlic, chopped
- ½ tsp each rosemary leaves
- ½ teaspoon sage leaves
- ½ teaspoon thyme leaves
- Salt to taste
- Pepper to taste
- 2 tablespoons flour
- ½ cup water

Instructions:

- Set the Instant Pot on sauté and add the turkey thighs.
- Brown them on all sides turning them every few minutes.
- Tip in the onions and garlic and sauté until brown.
- Add the mushrooms and herbs and mix well.
- Toss in the lemon juice and zest and mix well.
- Add the salt and pepper and mix well.
- Add the chicken broth and mix until well combined.
- Mix and cover the cooker.
- Cook on manual for 15 minutes.
- Serve hot with a sprinkling of parsley leaves on top.

Bacon Beans
Ingredients:

- 3 cups white beans
- 5 cups chicken broth
- 1/2 onion, chopped
- 1/2 cup bacon, chopped
- 2 tablespoons barbeque sauce
- 2 tablespoons ketchup
- 1/2 tablespoon honey
- Salt to taste
- Pepper to taste

Instructions:

- Rinse the beans and add to a bowl with enough water to cover.
- Meanwhile, add the bacon to the cooker and allow it to release oil.
- Add chopped onions and sauté till brown.
- Add the broth to the cooker and bring to a boil.
- Add the ketchup and honey and mix well.
- Add the salt and pepper and mix well.
- Toss in the beans and combine.
- Cover and cook on manual for 18 minutes.
- Serve hot with a sprinkling of parsley leaves on top.

Chapter 4: Soup Recipes

Beef Soup

Ingredients:

- 1 cup black eyed peas
- 1 large onion, chopped
- 2 garlic cloves, chopped
- 1 potato, chopped
- 2 carrots, chopped
- 1 celery stalk, chopped
- 1 cup beef, ground
- 2 cups beef broth
- 1 tablespoon Italian herb seasoning
- Salt to taste
- Pepper to taste
- Cilantro leaves to sprinkle

Instructions:

- Add the garlic and onion to the cooker and sauté until translucent.
- Tip in the potatoes, carrots and celery and mix well.
- Add the beef and mix until well combined.
- Tip in the beans, salt and pepper and mix well.
- Add the Italian seasoning and beef broth and mix until well combined.
- Cover the cooker and cook for 22 minutes.
- Serve hot with a sprinkling of cilantro leaves on top.

Potato Soup
Ingredients:

- 2 pounds' potatoes, chopped
- 2 carrots, chopped
- 2 cups vegetable stock
- 1/2 cup celery, chopped
- 1/2 cup spinach leaves, chopped
- 1 cup onion, chopped
- 1/8 teaspoon red pepper
- 1/8 teaspoon paprika powder
- 1 tablespoon flax seeds
- Salt to taste
- Parsley and basil to garnish

Instructions:

- Add the onion to the cooker and brown.
- Toss in the celery and sauté.
- Tip in the spinach leaves and allow them to release some water.
- Toss in the carrots and potatoes and mix well.
- Add the flax seeds, pepper and paprika and mix well.
- Add the salt and well combine.
- Tip in the vegetable stock and mix well.
- Cover and cook on manual for 25 minutes.
- Serve hot with a sprinkling of parsley and basil leaves on top.

Chinese Pork Soup
Ingredients:

- 2 large carrots, chopped
- 1 large radish, chopped
- 1 pork shank, chopped
- 4 cups water
- 1 ½ inch ginger, chopped
- 1 teaspoon lemon rind
- Salt to taste
- Pepper to taste
- Parsley leaves to sprinkle

Instructions:

- Add the water to the cooker and bring to a boil.
- Meanwhile, add the shank to a bowl along with the salt and pepper and rub it in.
- Add the ginger to the water along with the lemon rind and allow it to release flavor.
- Add the carrots and radish and mix until well combined.
- Add the shank and cover the cooker.
- Set on manual for 18 minutes.
- Serve hot with a sprinkling of parsley leaves on top.

Mixed Vegetable Soup
Ingredients:

- 1 cup celery, chopped
- 1/2 cup carrots, chopped
- 1 large onion, chopped
- 1 jalapeno, chopped
- Salt to taste
- Pepper to taste
- 2 tablespoons oil
- 1 teaspoon coriander seeds
- 1/2 teaspoon cumin seed
- 3 potatoes, chopped
- 3 cups chicken broth
- 2 cups of water
- ¼ teaspoon turmeric powder
- 1 teaspoon cumin powder
- Cilantro to sprinkle

Instructions:

- Set the cooker on sauté mode.
- Add the oil and allow it to warm up.
- Tip in the coriander and cumin seeds and allow them to splutter.
- Add the celery, carrots and onion along with the jalapenos and sauté for a few minutes.
- Toss in the turmeric and cumin and mix well.
- Add the potatoes and chicken broth and mix well.
- Cover and cook on manual for 22 minutes.
- Allow the pressure to release naturally.
- Serve hot with a sprinkling of cilantro leaves on top.

Bean Soup
Ingredients:

- 2 cups kidney beans
- 2 tablespoons sunflower seeds
- 1/2 cup of dry chestnuts
- 2 tablespoons lemon rind
- 4 tablespoons sugar
- 10 cups vegetable broth
- Parsley to sprinkle

Instructions:

- Add the sunflower seeds to the cooker along with the chestnuts and mix well.
- Add the lemon rind and sugar and mix.
- Toss in the sugar and kidney beans.
- Add the vegetable broth and well combine.
- Tip in the salt and pepper and mix well.
- Cover and cook on manual for 20 minutes.
- Serve hot with a sprinkling of parsley leaves on top.

Squash Soup

Ingredients:

- 1 large butternut squash, chopped
- 1 large onion, chopped
- 1-inch ginger, chopped
- 2 garlic cloves, chopped
- 4 cups vegetable broth
- 1 cup coconut milk
- Salt to taste
- Pepper to taste
- 2 tablespoons lemon juice
- 2 teaspoons curry powder
- ½ teaspoon turmeric powder
- 2 tablespoons olive oil
- Cilantro to sprinkle

Instructions:

- Add the oil to the cooker and allow it to heat up.
- Toss in the onion, garlic and ginger and sauté till brown.
- Tip in the salt, turmeric, curry powder and pepper and mix until well combined.
- Add the broth, coconut milk, and lemon juice and mix well.
- Add the squash and cover the cooker.
- Cook on manual for 15 minutes.
- Serve hot with a sprinkling of fresh cilantro on top.

Cauliflower Soup
Ingredients:

- 5 cups vegetable broth
- 1 whole cauliflower, chopped
- 2 cups potatoes, chopped
- 4 cups onion, chopped
- 2 large carrots, chopped
- 1 cup peas
- ½ cup celery stalks, chopped
- Salt to taste
- Pepper to taste
- Parsley to sprinkle

Instructions:

- Add the broth to the pot and bring to a boil.
- Toss in the onions and celery and mix well.
- Tip in the carrots, mushrooms, peas and potatoes and mix until well combined.
- Add the salt and pepper and mix well.
- Cover and cook on manual for 20 minutes.
- Serve hot with a sprinkling of parsley leaves on top.

Macaroni Soup
Ingredients:

- 1 large onion, chopped
- 2 celery stalks, chopped
- 5 cups chicken stock
- Salt to taste
- Pepper to taste
- 10 ounces' elbow macaroni
- 8 ounces' tomato sauce
- Parmesan cheese to sprinkle

Instructions:

- Add the stock to the cooker and set it on sauté.
- Toss in the onions and celery and allow the stock to come to a boil.
- Once done, add the salt and pepper and mix well.
- Tip in the chicken and mix.
- Add the tomato sauce and macaroni and mix until well combined.
- Close the cooker and cook for 15 minutes.
- Serve hot with a sprinkling of Parmesan cheese on top.

Chicken Noodle Soup
Ingredients:

- 4 chicken drumsticks
- 1 large onion, chopped
- 4 garlic cloves, chopped
- 5 mushrooms, chopped
- 1 large bay leaf
- 2 carrots, chopped
- 1 celery stalk, chopped
- 6 cups chicken stock
- 1 tablespoon olive oil
- 8 ounces' egg noodles
- Salt to taste
- Pepper to taste
- Lemon juice to drizzle
- Cilantro leaves to sprinkle

Instructions:

- Press the sauté button and add the oil.
- Allow it to heat up before tossing in the onions and garlic.
- Sauté until brown.
- Add the mushrooms and brown them.
- Toss in the salt and pepper and mix well.
- At this point the mushrooms will start sweating.
- Add the bay leaf and carrots along with the celery and mix.
- Add the chicken stock to deglaze the cooker.
- Mix until well combined.
- Add the chicken drumsticks to the cooker and mix until well combined.

- Cook on high heat for 10 minutes.
- Allow the pressure to release naturally.
- Once done, add the noodles and mix well.
- Cook for a further 10 minutes.
- Cut and squeeze in the lemon.
- Serve with a sprinkling of cilantro leaves on top.

Bone Broth

Ingredients:

- 5 cups water
- 1 teaspoon vinegar
- 1 large onion, chopped
- ½ inch ginger, chopped
- 1 cup mushrooms of your choice
- 4 pounds' bones (meat of your choice)
- Lemon to drizzle
- Cilantro to sprinkle

Instructions:

- Add the bone to the cooker along with the Vinegar and water and mix until well combined.
- Allow it to come to a boil.
- Toss in the onions, mushrooms and garlic and mix well.
- Close the cooker and set on manual 15 minutes.
- Once done, allow the steam to escape naturally.
- Drain it to remove any froth.
- Serve hot with a drizzle of lemon and a sprinkling of cilantro leaves on top.

Chapter 5: Vegetarian Recipes

Vegetable Bean Pilaf
Ingredients:

- 1 large onion, chopped
- 1 carrot, chopped
- 1 sweet potato, chopped
- 1 cup green lentils
- 1 teaspoon thyme leaves
- 1 bay leaf
- 1/2 teaspoon rosemary, chopped
- 2 cups vegetable stock
- 1 cup rice
- 1 tablespoon Worcestershire sauce
- 1 cup tomatoes, chopped
- Parsley to sprinkle

Instructions:

- Add the onion to the cooker and brown.
- Toss in the carrots and sauté.
- Add the sweet potatoes, lentils and mix well.
- Add the thyme and bay leaves and mix.
- Add the vegetable stock, Worcestershire sauce and mix.
- Add the rice and mix well.
- Add the tomatoes and combine.
- Cover and cook on manual for 20 minutes.
- Serve warm with a sprinkling of fresh parsley leaves on top.

Vegetable Dumplings
Ingredients:

- 1 tablespoon olive oil
- 1 cup mushrooms
- 1 cup cabbage
- ½ cup carrot, chopped
- 2 tablespoons soya sauce
- 1 tablespoon vinegar
- 1 teaspoon fresh ginger
- ½ cup vegetable stock
- 12 around vegan dumpling wrappers

Instructions:

- Add the oil to the cooker and allow it to heat up.
- Add the mushrooms and cabbage and mix until well combined.
- Add the carrots, soya sauce, vinegar and ginger and mix well.
- Add vegetable stock to it and cover the cooker.
- Meanwhile, prepare the dumpling wrappers.
- Once the carrots cook out use a spoon to add it to the center of the dumpling wrappers.
- Add water to the cooker and place a trivet on top.
- Add the dumplings to the steamer basket and place it on the trivet.
- Steam for 10 minutes.
- Serve hot.

Asian Brussels Sprouts
Ingredients:

- 2 pounds Brussels sprouts
- 5 tablespoons soya sauce
- 2 tablespoons sriracha sauce
- 1 tablespoon rice vinegar
- 2 tablespoons sesame oil
- 4 strips bacon, chopped
- 1 tablespoon almonds, chopped
- 1 teaspoon red pepper flakes
- 5 garlic cloves, chopped
- 1 onion, chopped
- 1 tablespoon paprika
- Salt to taste
- Pepper to taste
- Cilantro leaves to sprinkle

Instructions:

- Add the sesame oil to the cooker and heat.
- Toss in the bacon and sauté.
- Add the onions and garlic and brown it.
- Toss in the paprika, salt and pepper and mix well.
- Add the soya sauce, sriracha sauce, and vinegar and mix until well combined.
- Add the Brussels sprouts, almonds and mix.
- Cover and cook on manual for 20 minutes.
- Serve warm with a sprinkling of fresh cilantro leaves on top.

Cauliflower Rice

Ingredients:

- 1 cauliflower, chopped
- 2 tablespoons olive oil
- Salt to taste
- Pepper to taste
- ½ teaspoon parsley
- 1 teaspoon cumin seeds
- ¼ teaspoon turmeric powder
- ¼ teaspoon paprika
- Cilantro to sprinkle

Instructions:

- Add the oil to the cooker and allow it to heat up.
- Add the cumin seeds, paprika and turmeric and mix well.
- Add the cauliflower to a grinder and grind into a coarse powder.
- Add it to the cooker along with water and cover.
- Cook on manual for 10 minutes.
- Serve warm with a sprinkling of fresh cilantro leaves on top.

Mushroom Risotto
Ingredients:

- 1 large onion, chopped
- 3 garlic cloves, chopped
- 1 tablespoon olive oil
- 4 ounces' mushrooms, chopped
- Salt to taste
- Pepper to taste
- 1 teaspoon thyme leaves
- 1/2 cup dry wine
- 3 cups vegetable broth
- 1 cup Arborio rice
- 1/4 cup lemon juice
- 2 cups fresh spinach
- 1 tablespoon butter
- Cilantro to sprinkle

Instructions:

- Add the oil to the cooker along with the onion and garlic and sauté.
- Toss in the mushrooms and salt and pepper and mix well.
- Allow the mushrooms to sweat before adding in the thyme leaves. 'Add the dry wine along with the vegetable broth.
- Add the Arborio rice and stir.
- Toss in the butter and spinach and cover the cooker.
- Cook on manual for 20 minutes.
- Serve warm with a sprinkling of fresh cilantro leaves on top.

Cottage Cheese Kebab
Ingredients:

- 1 cup cottage cheese
- 1 cup bread crumbs
- 1 teaspoon cumin powder
- 1 tablespoon ground almonds
- Salt to taste
- Pepper to taste
- 1 large onion, chopped
- 1-inch ginger, minced
- 4 chilies
- 1 egg
- 1 tablespoon vegetable oil

Instructions:

- Add the cheese to a bowl along with the breadcrumbs, salt and pepper and mix well.
- Add the ginger and onion and mix well.
- Toss in the chilies and egg and mix until well combined.
- Make small rounds out of the mixture.
- Heat oil in the cooker and add the rounds.
- Cook for 20 minutes.
- Serve hot.

Potatoes And Mushroom
Ingredients:

- 1 pound mushrooms, chopped
- 1 cup water
- 2 pounds' beans
- 2 pounds' potatoes, chopped
- Salt to taste
- Pepper to taste
- 3 eggs
- ¼ cup cheese

Instructions:

- Add the mushrooms to the cooker and allow them to sweat.
- Add the potatoes and beans and sauté.
- Add the salt and pepper and mix well.
- Add the eggs and cheese and mix.
- Cover and cook for 15 minutes.
- Serve warm.

Instant Pot Hummus
Ingredients:

- 1 cup chickpeas
- 1 bay leaf
- 4 garlic cloves, chopped
- 2 tablespoons tahini
- 1 lemon, juiced and zested
- ¼ teaspoon cumin powder
- Salt to taste
- Pepper to taste
- ½ bunch Parsley, chopped
- Paprika to taste
- 1 tablespoon extra-virgin olive oil

Instructions:

- Add the oil to the cooker and toss in the garlic and sauté.
- Add the bay leaf.
- Add the cumin, lemon, tahini, salt and pepper and mix well.
- Add the chickpeas and paprika and mix.
- Add the parsley and mix in
- Add 1-cup water and cover.
- Cook on manual for 20 minutes.
- Allow to cool down. Add to a blender and whizz until smooth.
- Serve with a sprinkling of cilantro on top.

Vegetable Stew
Ingredients:

- 1 leek, halved
- 2 mushroom chopped
- 1 teaspoon vegetable oil
- 6 carrots, chopped
- 3 potatoes, chopped
- 2 celery ribs, chopped
- 1 onion, chopped
- 1 cup peas
- 4 cups water
- 1 teaspoon Italian seasoning
- Salt to taste
- Pepper to taste
- Cilantro to sprinkle

Instructions:

- Add the oil to the cooker and warm it up.
- Toss in the onion and celery and brown it.
- Add the potatoes and carrots and sauté.
- Toss in the peas and Italian seasoning along with the salt and pepper and mix well.
- Add the water and mix well.
- Cover and cook on high for 20 minutes.
- Serve warm with a sprinkling of fresh cilantro leaves on top.

Stuffed Bell Peppers
Ingredients:

- 5 bell peppers
- 1-pound beef, minced
- 1 large onion, Chopped
- 1 cup tomatoes, chopped
- ½ cup rice
- 1 cup water
- Salt to taste
- 1 cup cheese

Instructions:

- Remove the tops of the peppers and use a sharp knife to remove the seeds and membranes.
- Add the beef to a bowl along with the onion and tomatoes and mix.
- Toss in the rice and salt and mix.
- Stuff each of the peppers with this and sprinkle the cheese on top.
- Cover the top with their tops.
- Add oil to the cooker and place the peppers in it.
- Cover and cook for 10 minutes.
- Serve hot.

Chapter 6: Side Dishes

Sweet potato dip
Ingredients:

- 3 sweet potatoes
- 1 cup water
- Salt to taste
- Pepper to taste
- 1 tablespoon paprika
- 1 lemon, juiced
- Cilantro leaves

Instructions:

- Cut the sweet potato into cubes and add to the cooker along with the water.
- Cook on manual for 20 minutes.
- Allow it to cool naturally.
- Meanwhile, add the pepper, salt and paprika to a bowl along with the lemon juice and mix well.
- Add the sweet potato to a bowl and mash it.
- Add the lemon juice on top and serve.

Instant Pot Mixed Beans Stew
Ingredients:

- 2 pounds mixed beans
- 1 large onion, chopped
- 5 garlic cloves, chopped
- 1 jalapeno, chopped
- 2 teaspoons oregano leaves
- 2 teaspoons cumin powder
- Salt to taste
- Pepper to taste
- 3 tablespoons butter
- 4 cups vegetable broth
- 4 cups water
- Parsley leaves to sprinkle

Instructions:

- Add the butter to the cooker and allow it to heat up.
- Add the garlic and onions and sauté.
- Toss in the jalapenos and oregano and mix well.
- Add the salt and pepper and mix.
- Add the cumin powder and mix.
- Add the beans and mix.
- Pour in the water and vegetable stock and mix until well combined.
- Cover the cooker and cook on manual for 15 minutes.
- Serve warm with a sprinkling of fresh parsley leaves on top.

Cabbage And Sausage
Ingredients:

- 1-pound turkey sausage, chopped
- 1 cabbage, chopped
- 1 onion, chopped
- 3 garlic cloves, chopped
- 2 teaspoons brown sugar
- 2 teaspoons balsamic vinegar
- 2 teaspoons Dijon mustard
- 1 tablespoon olive oil
- 1 cup vegetable stock
- Salt to taste
- Pepper to taste
- Cilantro leaves

Instructions:

- Add the oil to the cooker and toss in the onions.
- Allow it to sauté before adding in the sausages.
- Add the garlic and brown.
- Add the sugar, vinegar and mustard and mix well.
- Tip in the cabbage and mix until well combined.
- Add the vegetable stock and mix everything.
- Cover and cook on manual for 20 minutes.
- Serve warm with a sprinkling of fresh cilantro leaves on top.

Corn Chowder
Ingredients:

- 5 ears of corn
- 5 tablespoons butter
- 1 large onion, chopped
- 3 cups water
- 2 potatoes, chopped
- 2 tablespoons corn flour
- 2 tablespoons water
- 3 cups milk
- 1 /8 teaspoon paprika
- Salt to taste
- Pepper to taste
- Parsley leaves to sprinkle

Instructions:

- Add the butter to the cooker and allow it to melt.
- Add the chopped onion and sauté till brown.
- Add the potatoes and sauté.
- Add the corn, milk, and paprika and mix until well combined.
- Add the salt and pepper and mix well.
- Add the corn flour to a bowl along with the water and make a paste.
- Add it in and mix well.
- Cover and cook on manual for 20 minutes.
- Serve warm with a sprinkling of fresh parsley leaves on top.

Parsnips And Cream
Ingredients:

- 1/4 cup butter
- 2 pounds' parsnips
- Salt to taste
- Pepper to taste
- 2 tablespoons thyme
- 1 tablespoon rosemary
- 2 cups vegetable broth
- 5 tablespoons cream
- 2 tablespoon cilantro leaves

Instructions:

- Press sauté on the Instant Pot and add the butter to it.
- Add the parsnips, salt and pepper and allow it to brown on all sides.
- Add the thyme and rosemary and mix until well combined.
- Add the broth and mix until well combined.
- Cover and cook on manual for 20 minutes.
- Meanwhile, add the cream to a bowl along with the cilantro and mix until well combined.
- Serve the parsnips with the creamy dip.

Carrot Puree
Ingredients:

- 2 pounds' carrot
- 1 tablespoon butter
- 1 tablespoon honey
- Salt to taste
- Pepper to taste
- 1 cup water
- 2 tablespoons brown sugar

Instructions:

- Add the carrots and water to the cooker and cover.
- Cook on manual for 20 minutes.
- Once done, remove and drain the
- Add the butter to the cooker along with the salt pepper and honey and mix until well combined.
- Toss in the sugar and water and mix well.
- Add the carrots and mix until well combined.
- Cover and cook for 5 minutes.
- Once done, add to a blender and make a puree.

Spicy Beets
Ingredients:

- 1 pound beetroots
- 1 cup water
- 1/4 cup honey
- 2 tablespoons butter
- 2 teaspoons mustard paste
- 1 teaspoon cumin powder
- 1 teaspoon paprika powder
- 2 teaspoons garlic, chopped
- 1 tablespoon hot sauce
- Salt to taste
- Pepper to taste
- Toasted sesame to sprinkle

Instructions:

- Chop the beetroots lengthwise into long strips.
- Add the water to the cooker and bring to a boil.
- Toss in the beetroots and cover.
- Cook on manual for 20 minutes.
- Add the honey to a bowl along with the cumin, paprika and hot sauce and mix until well combined.
- Drain the cooker and remove the beetroots.
- Add the butter and warm it up before tossing in the garlic and browning.
- Add the beetroots along with the honey mixture.
- Add the mustard and mix until well combined.
- Add salt and pepper and mix well.
- Cover the cooker and cook for 5 minutes.
- Serve hot with a sprinkling of toasted sesame seeds on top.

Roasted Potatoes
Ingredients:

- 5 tablespoon vegetable oil
- 2 pounds' potatoes
- 1 tablespoon rosemary
- 4 garlic cloves, chopped
- ½ cup Stock
- Salt to taste
- Pepper to taste
- Cilantro leaves to sprinkle

Instructions:

- Add the oil to the cooker and toss in the garlic.
- Allow it to brown before adding in the salt and pepper.
- Add the potatoes and sauté.
- Add the stock and mix well.
- Cover cooker and cook the potatoes on manual for 10 minutes.
- Serve warm with a sprinkling of fresh cilantro leaves on top.

Glazed Brussels
Ingredients:

- 2 pounds Brussels sprouts
- ½ cup orange juice
- 1 teaspoon orange zest
- 1 tablespoon butter
- 2 tablespoons honey
- Salt to taste
- Pepper to taste

Instructions:

- Put the cooker on sauté and add the butter and sprouts.
- Mix in the orange juice and zest and mix well.
- Add the salt and pepper along with the honey and mix well.
- Cook on manual for 20 minutes.
- Serve hot.

Prune Mash
Ingredients:

- 10 ounces' prunes
- 2 apples, chopped
- 1 cup water
- ¼ cup lemon juice
- ½ cup honey
- Salt to taste
- Pepper to taste
- 1 teaspoon nutmeg

Instructions:

- Add the water to the cooker and allow it to boil. Toss in the prunes and apples and cover the cooker.
- Cook on manual for 20 minutes.
- Meanwhile add the lemon juice and honey to a bowl and mix until well combined.
- Add the salt and pepper and mix well.
- Add the nutmeg and combine.
- Once the apples are done, add them to a bowl along with the prunes and mash.
- Mix it in with the honey and lemon and mix well.
- Serve as a dip.

Chapter 7: Snack Recipes

Spicy Sticky Chicken Wings
Ingredients:

- 3 pounds Chicken Wings
- 2 tablespoons soya sauce
- 1/2 cup Honey
- ¼ cup fish sauce
- 1 teaspoon Sesame Oil
- 5 garlic cloves, chopped
- 3 tablespoons ginger, chopped
- ½ teaspoon chili paste
- ¼ cup water
- Parsley to sprinkle

Instructions:

- Add the soya sauce to a bowl along with the honey and fish sauce and mix until well combined.
- Add the sesame oil to the cooker and allow it to heat up.
- Toss in the garlic and ginger and sauté till brown.
- Add the chili paste and mix well.
- Dip the chicken in the honey sauce and add to the cooker.
- Pour any remaining into it along with the water.
- Mix until well combined and close the cooker.
- Cook for 20 minutes on manual.
- Serve hot with a sprinkling of fresh parsley leaves on top.

Sesame Noodles
Ingredients:

- 15 ounces' egg noodles
- 3 cups Water
- 8 Scallions, chopped
- 3 tablespoons sesame oil
- 1/2 cup soya sauce
- 10 garlic cloves, chopped
- 5 tablespoons vinegar
- 5 tablespoons sugar
- 1 teaspoon chili oil
- Spring onions to sprinkle

Instructions:

- Add the water to the cooker along with the noodles and boil it.
- Strain the same.
- Add the oil to a cooker along with the scallions and brown.
- Add the garlic and brown.
- Add the vinegar and sugar and mix until well combined.
- Add the chili oil, salt and pepper and mix well.
- Add the noodles and cover.
- Cook on manual for 20 minutes.
- Serve hot with a sprinkling of fresh spring onion leaves on top.

Pasta Salad
Ingredients:

- 8 bacon slices
- 1-pound macaroni Pasta
- Salt to taste
- Pepper to taste
- 3 cups water
- ½ cup Mayonnaise
- ¼ cup yogurt
- 2 teaspoons lemon juice
- 1 teaspoon sugar
- 2 teaspoons Worcestershire sauce
- Cilantro to sprinkle

Instructions:

- Add the water to the cooker and bring it to a boil before adding in the macaroni.
- Allow it to soften.
- Meanwhile, add the mayonnaise and yogurt to a bowl along with the lemon juice, salt and pepper and mix until well combined.
- Add the sugar and Worcestershire sauce and mix well.
- Add chopped bacon to it and mix well.
- Once the macaroni is done, drain it out.
- Add it to the yogurt and mix well.
- Serve warm with a sprinkling of fresh cilantro leaves on top.

Spicy Eggplants
Ingredients:

- 2 large eggplants, chopped
- Salt to taste
- Pepper to taste
- 1 tablespoon chili powder
- 1 tablespoon curry powder
- 2 tablespoons vegetable oil
- 1 garlic clove, minced
- ½ cup water
- Parsley leaves to sprinkle

Instructions:

- Add the oil to the cooker and heat it up.
- Add the garlic and sauté till brown.
- Add the eggplants and brown all around.
- Add the chili powder, curry powder, salt and pepper and mix well.
- Add the water and mix until well combined.
- Cook on manual for 20 minutes.
- Serve warm with a sprinkling of fresh cilantro leaves on top.

Glazed Shallots
Ingredients:

- 1 pound shallots
- 1 tablespoon oil
- ½ cup water
- Salt to taste
- Pepper to taste
- 4 tablespoons balsamic vinegar
- 1 tablespoon honey
- 1 tablespoon flour

Instructions:

- Mix the honey and vinegar in a bowl.
- Add the salt and pepper and mix until well combined.
- Add the flour and mix well.
- Add the oil to the cooker and toss in the onions.
- Mix well until slightly brown.
- Add the water and cover the cooker.
- Cook on high for 10 minutes.
- Serve hot.

Crispy Potatoes
Ingredients:

- 2 cups potatoes, cubed
- 1 tablespoon olive oil
- Salt to taste
- Pepper to taste
- 1/2 teaspoon turmeric powder
- 1 tablespoon chili powder
- 2 teaspoons lemon juice
- Cilantro to sprinkle

Instructions:

- Add the oil to the cooker and allow it to heat up.
- Add the potatoes and brown them on all sides.
- Add the salt and pepper and mix well.
- Tip in the turmeric and chili powder and combine.
- Add the lemon juice and mix.
- Cover the cooker and cook for 5 minutes.
- Serve hot with a sprinkling of fresh spring onion leaves on top.

Instant Pot Szechuan Chicken
Ingredients:

- 3 pounds' chicken breasts, chopped
- 1 cup corn flour
- 2 tablespoons Szechuan peppercorns, powdered
- 2 Eggs
- 2 Tablespoons peanut oil
- 1 Tablespoon ginger, chopped
- 1 Tablespoon garlic, chopped

Sauce

- 1/4 cup rice wine
- 1/4 cup Brown Sugar
- 1/4 cup dark soya sauce
- 2 teaspoons chili paste
- 1 cup chicken stock
- Spring onion to sprinkle

Instructions:

- Add the corn flour to a bowl along with the peppercorns and mix well.
- Add the eggs to a bowl along with the ginger and garlic and mix well.
- Add the oil to the cooker and allow it to heat up.
- Dip the chicken in the egg mixture followed by the flour mix and add to the oil.
- Brown the chicken on all sides and take it out.
- Add the rice wine, brown sugar, chili paste, soya sauce and chicken stock to the cooker and mix until well combined.
- Add the chicken pieces to it and mix well.

- Cover and cook for 5 minutes.
- Serve hot with a sprinkling of fresh spring onion leaves on top.

Mustard Chicken

Ingredients:

- 1 tablespoon olive oil
- 2 pounds' chicken breasts
- 1 cup mustard paste
- ⅓ cup honey
- Salt to taste
- Pepper to taste
- 1 large onion, chopped
- 1 cup chicken stock

Instructions:

- Add the mustard and honey to a bowl and mix well.
- Add the salt and pepper and mix until well combined.
- Add the oil and onion to the cooker and sauté till brown.
- Add the chicken and roast on all sides.
- Add the mustard mix to the chicken and tip in the chicken stock.
- Cover and cook for 15 minutes.
- Serve hot.

Corn Chili
Ingredients:

- 3 tablespoons olive oil
- 2 large onions, chopped
- 1 bell pepper, chopped
- 2 jalapeños, chopped
- 2 garlic cloves, chopped
- 2 teaspoons cumin powder
- 1 tablespoon chili powder
- 1 teaspoon oregano
- Salt to taste
- Pepper to taste
- 2 pounds' beef mince
- 2cup tomatoes, chopped
- 1 cup fava beans
- 1 cup kidney beans
- 2 cups beef stock
- Parsley leaves to sprinkle

Instructions:

- Press the sauté button on the cooker.
- Add the oil and mix in the beef.
- Allow it to brown.
- Toss in the onions and bell peppers along with the jalapenos and mix well.
- Add the garlic, cumin and chili powder along with the oregano, salt and pepper and mix until well combined.
- Add the beans, tomatoes and beef stock and mix well.
- Close and cook on manual for 25 minutes.
- Serve hot with a sprinkling of fresh parsley leaves on top.

Chapter 8: All Natural Desserts

Instant Pot Mango Cheesecake
Ingredients:

- 2 eggs
- ½ cup sugar
- 1 cup mango puree
- 15 ounces' cream cheese
- 1 teaspoon nutmeg powder

Crust

- 2 cups crackers, crushed
- ¼ cup butter
- ½ cup mango, chopped

Instructions:

- Crush the crackers by adding to a blender or using a rolling pin.
- Add it to a bowl along with the butter and mix until well combined.
- Pour the mix into a mold and press it down gently so as to cover the bottom and the sides.
- Place it in the freezer to set the base a little.
- In the meantime, add the eggs to a bowl and beat on high.

- Add the mango puree, and cheese and beat until well combined.
- Add the nutmeg and sugar and mix until well combined.
- Pour it over the base.
- Add water to the cooker and place the trivet.
- Use an aluminum foil to create a sling for the cooker by folding it in half and placing it over the trivet such that the sides rise above the mold.
- Place the mold over the sling and cover the cooker.
- Cook on manual for 25 minutes.
- Remove and allow the cake to cool down completely before sprinkling mango pieces on top.

Chocolate Pudding
Ingredients:

- 1 cup flour
- 2 teaspoons baking powder
- Pinch of salt
- ½ cup butter
- 1/2 cup granulated sugar
- 1 small egg
- 4 ounces' milk
- 1/4-pound chocolate chips
- 1 cup cream

Instructions:

- Add the chocolate and cream to a double boiler and allow it to melt completely.
- Meanwhile, add the flour, baking powder and salt to a sieve and mix well.
- Tip in the butter and sugar and mix until well combined.
- Add the egg and milk and mix well.
- Add the melted chocolate and mix until well combined.
- Add water and trivet to the cooker.
- Use an aluminum foil to fold and act as a sling.
- Place it into the cooker and place the mold over it.
- Steam on manual for 25 minutes.
- Allow it to cool down before serving.

Carrot Cake
Ingredients:

- 2 cups water
- 4 large carrots
- 2 tablespoons lemon juice
- ½ teaspoon vanilla extract
- ½ cup flour
- ⅓ cup coconut flour
- ½ teaspoon baking powder
- ¼ cup butter
- Pinch of salt
- 3/4 cup sugar
- 2 tablespoons powdered sugar

Instructions:

- Add the water to a pan and toss in chopped carrots to soften up a little.
- Once done, add to a blender and make a smooth paste.
- Add the flours and baking powder along with the salt to a sieve and add to a bowl.
- Mix the butter and sugar together and cream until well combined.
- Add the lemon juice, vanilla and mix well.
- Tip in the carrot puree along with the flour and fold the mixture.
- Grease a mold or add a parchment paper to a mold and pour in the mixture.
- Add water to the cooker and place a trivet.
- Use an aluminum foil to make a sling.
- Place the mold over the sling.

- Cook on manual for 25 minutes.
- Allow it to cool down completely before sifting powdered sugar on top.

Choco Lava Cake
Ingredients:

- 1 egg, beaten
- 2 tablespoons butter, melted
- 5 tablespoons sugar
- 5 tablespoons milk
- 5 tablespoons flour
- 1 tablespoon cocoa powder
- ½ teaspoon salt
- ½ teaspoon baking powder
- ½ teaspoon orange zest
- 2-3 pieces of whole chocolate

Instructions:

- Add butter and flour to ramekins to grease.
- Add the butter and sugar to a bowl and cream them together.
- Mix in the milk and orange and whizz until well combined.
- Add the flour, cocoa powder, baking powder and salt to a sieve and mix it into the wet ingredients.
- Fold them together.
- Pour the batter into the ramekins 3/4ths way up.
- Insert one piece of chocolate between each of them.
- Add water to the cooker and place the trivet on top.
- Bake the ramekins for 5 minutes on high.
- Allow it to cool down before serving warm.

Carrot Pudding
Ingredients:

- 2 large carrots
- ½ cup milk
- ½ cup sugar
- 2 tablespoons clarified butter
- 10 almonds, chopped
- 10 cashews, chopped
- 10 whole raisins
- 2 cardamom pods, crushed

Recipe:

- Add the butter to the pot and allow it to heat up.
- Add in the almonds, cashews and raisins and sauté for 2 minutes.
- Tip in the carrots and mix until combined.
- Add in the sugar, milk and cardamom and mix well.
- Cover and cook on manual for 15 minutes.
- Cool and serve.

Instant Pot Apple Crisp
Ingredients:

- 5 apples, chopped
- 2 teaspoons cinnamon powder
- 1/2 tsp nutmeg powder
- 1/2 cup water
- 1 tablespoon honey
- 5 tablespoons butter
- 3/4 cups oats
- 1/4 cup flour
- 1/4 cup brown sugar
- 1/2 tsp salt

Instructions:

- Add the apples to the Instant Pot and sprinkle the cinnamon and nutmeg powder on top.
- Add the water and honey and mix.
- Add the butter to a bowl along with the oats, flour, sugar and salt and mix well.
- Add this over the apples.
- Close the cooker and select manual 8 minutes.
- Allow the pressure to escape naturally.
- Serve warm.

Walnut Banana Cake
Ingredients:

- 2 cups all-purpose flour
- 2 ripe bananas, mashed
- 1 teaspoon vanilla extract
- 2 eggs, beaten
- 5 tablespoons butter
- ½ cup milk
- 1 tablespoon lemon juice
- 1 teaspoon baking powder
- 1/2 teaspoon cinnamon
- 1/3 cup walnuts, chopped
- ¼ cup powdered sugar

Instructions:

- Cream the butter and sugar together.
- Add the vanilla, lemon juice and milk and mix until well combined.
- Add mashed banana and mix well.
- Add the flour, baking powder, and cinnamon to a sieve.
- Mix this into the batter and fold.
- Fold in the chopped walnuts.
- Grease cake molds and pour the cake batter into it.
- Add water to the cooker and use foil to make a sling.
- Place the mold on top.
- Cook on manual for 25 minutes.
- Allow it to cool down before serving hot.

Vermicelli Pudding
Ingredients:

- 1 tablespoon almonds, chopped
- 1 tablespoon cashews, chopped
- 1 tablespoon raisins
- 2 cardamom pods
- ½ teaspoon nutmeg
- 1/4-inch cinnamon bark, powdered
- 2 tablespoons clarified butter
- 2 1/4 cups milk
- 2 cups water
- 1 cup vermicelli
- 2 cups sugar
- 1 tablespoon vanilla extract
- ½ teaspoon salt

Instructions:

- Add the butter to the cooker and allow it to heat up before adding in the almonds and cashews.
- Add the raisins and cardamom, nutmeg along with the cinnamon and mix well.
- Toss in the vermicelli and water and let it come to a boil.
- Add the milk and sugar and mix well.
- Add the vanilla extract along with the salt and mix well.
- Cover and cook on manual for 25 minutes.
- Serve warm.

Baked Apples
Ingredients:

- 3 small apples, peeled
- 10 to 12 cloves
- 5 tablespoons brown sugar
- 2 tablespoons butter

Instructions:

- Mix the butter and sugar together and set aside.
- Core the apples using a coring device or a sharp knife.
- Insert cloves all around the apples.
- Fill them up with the butter and sugar.
- Add water to the cooker and place the trivet.
- Place the apples on top.
- Cook on manual for 25 minutes.
- Serve warm.

Sweet Yogurt
Ingredients:

- 2 cups strawberries
- 2 tablespoons lemon juice
- 1 cup sugar
- 2 cups Instant Pot yogurt

Instructions:

- Add the strawberries to a bowl along with the lemon juice and mix well.
- Add the yogurt and sugar to a bowl and mix until well combined.
- Add the yogurt and strawberry mix to the Instant Pot and cook on manual for 25 minutes.
- Allow it to cool down before serving.

Chocolate Orange Cake
Ingredients:

- 6 ounces' chocolate
- 2 cups orange juice and pulp
- ½ cup butter
- 1 cup flour
- 1½ teaspoons vanilla extract
- ⅓ cup cocoa powder
- ½ teaspoon salt
- 1/2 cup honey

Instructions:

- Add water to the cooker and place the trivet on top.
- Use aluminum foil to create a sling and place over the trivet.
- Add the butter to a double boiler and toss in the chocolate.
- Get them to melt.
- Add the honey to the mix and combine.
- Add the flour, cocoa powder, salt and mix well.
- Grease a mold or add parchment paper and pour the mixture on top.
- Add mold to the cooker and pick manual 25 minutes.
- Allow it to cool down before serving.

Pressure Tips: Tips & Techniques Help You Master Your Skills

The Instant Pot is quite versatile and here are some of its uses.

- The Instant Pot serves as a slow cooker. A slow cooker basically cooks food at a slower pace. This ensures the nutritional value is maintained. You can add all the ingredients and wait for the cooker to cook it at its own pace. You can have a ready meal in 6 to 8 hours. This is great to make breakfast and also dinner.
- At the same time, the cooker also serves as a pressure cooker. It heats up the water to a high temperature and cooks the food at a rapid pace. This can help you cut down on a lot of time. But don't think it will compromise on the nutrition or flavor, as both will be preserved.
- The Instant Pot makes for a great rice cooker. In fact, it looks like one as well. You can add the rice and water and pick the right setting for it. The rice will be ready in 5 to 10 minutes. You can also use it to make pilaf, fried rice etc.
- The Instant Pot doubles up as a steamer. You can steam foods such as dumplings, rice cakes etc.
- The sauté feature of the cooker is unique and convenient. You can use it to sauté the ingredients before cooking them.
- You can use the cooker to keep your foods warm. You can add a dish to the cooker and reheat it.

- The cooker also serves as a yogurt maker. In fact, there happens to be a preset setting on the cooker that can be used to make the yogurt.
- Go through the instructional manual provided by the company so that you know how your Instant Pot operates. They might also provide tips and tricks to cook foods faster.
- You can use the manual button provided on the cooker to change the timing. As you know, the cooker comes with certain preset settings that you can choose to cook foods faster. But you can also change it to manual settings to cook food for a specific time. This is a great feature for all those that wish to cook foods for other recipes.
- If you wish to cook using the Instant Pot on a regular basis, then look for a bigger model. You will be able to cook more food in it.
- The Instant Pot comes with two release options namely the quick release and the natural release. The quick release helps you release the steam with ease. All you have to do is press the button and release the steam naturally. The natural release releases the steam naturally. Although it might take a little more time for the steam to escape naturally, it will be best to use this option. Forcing the steam out can sometimes result in the foods not cooking properly.
- Remember that the Instant Pot does not use too much liquid. You must try to limit it to just one cup so that your foods can cook evenly. If you add more, then you might end up with a watery dish.
- If your meal does end up getting runny then use thickeners to balance it out. You can use corn flour, all-purpose flour and gram flour as these can all be

used as thickening agents. Add it to a bowl with a little water and add to the dish to thicken it.

- The sauté function of the Instant Pot is a great feature to brown ingredients. Right from meats to vegetables, you can add them in and brown them. The sauté button is provided as a preset option on the machine.
- You can deglaze the cooker after sautéing. Just add water or stock to it in order to loosen it up a little. The same can be converted into a sauce or gravy.
- The lid of the cooker can sometimes get hot and you must be careful while opening it. Doing it too fast can result in some of the hot condensation water getting onto your hand. In such a case, the safest way to open it will be to hold it at an angle and lift it up. That way, the water will not fall on your hands. You can also use gloves if you wish to be extra careful.
- It is possible for you to cook two dishes at once. You can add ingredients to the bottom of the cooker to cook them and also in a bowl or steamer. That way, you will be able to cook more recipes at once.
- A neat trick to get more out of your foods is by soaking it in advance. Try to soak rice, beans, lentils and other dry ingredients so that you can cut down on the cooking time. Try to soak it for 4 to 5 hours as that will help the foods swell up and cook faster.
- The Instant Pot is a savior for all those that are in a hurry to cook. You do not have to worry about thawing your foods as they can directly go into the cooker. They will thaw in the cooker as you cook them.
- You have to clean up the cooker and its components as soon as you are finished. This will help the cooker last longer and you will be able to use it for your next recipe.

- If you are a regular user of the cooker, then it will be best to buy good quality utensils and ladles to use with the cooker. Although the company will supply quality ones, having spare ones will work well for regular users.
- Although the cooker is extremely safe to operate, it is important not to force it open. Doing so can cause you to sustain injury. You must use the quick release option to release steam if you do not wish for it to cool down naturally.
- The gasket is one of the most important components of the cooker. You must ensure that it is kept safe and away from damage. Check it on a regular basis to ensure that it is in good clean state.
- Do not try to fix the cooker by yourself if it is not functioning optimally. Doing so can cause you to worsen the problem. Take it to an authorized dealer to have it checked.

The Instant Pot can be used to make yogurt. The pot can be used to make both natural and Greek yogurt. Here is a recipe for both.

Yogurt
Ingredients:

- 1 Gallon Milk
- 2 Tablespoons yogurt with active culture
- Digital Thermometer

Instructions:

- Start by sterilizing the cooker. Add water to it and steam it for 10 minutes.
- Discard the water once it is done.
- Add the milk to the cooker and close it.
- Now press the yogurt button on the cooker followed by the boil button.
- Uncover every 5 minutes to gently whisk the milk using a steel whisk.
- Allow it to come to a boil.
- Meanwhile, add ice cubes and water to a tub or a sink.
- Check the temperature of the milk to see if it has reached 180 degrees.
- If it has then place it in the cold water and continue whisking it.
- Use the thermometer to check if the temperature has reached 110 degrees.
- If it has, then add the yogurt culture and whisk further.
- Pour this back into the cooker and cover it.
- Choose the yogurt option and allow it to cook for 10 hours.
- The next day, check if the yogurt is set.

Greek Yogurt

Greek yogurt can be prepared by draining away the whey from the Greek yogurt. Here are the steps to follow for the same.

- Add the Greek yogurt to a sieve and allow all the whey to drain.
- Once done, transfer it to a muslin cloth to further thicken it.

Conclusion

Thank you again for purchasing this book!

I hope this book was able to help you to understand how an Instant Pot works. The next step is to start preparing the recipes and feed your near and dear ones with the food you have prepared in it. You can try all the recipes mentioned in this book.

Finally, if you enjoyed this book, then I'd like to ask you for a favor, would you be kind enough to leave a review for this book on Amazon? It'd be greatly appreciated!

Thank you and good luck!

17839408R00085

Printed in Poland
by Amazon Fulfillment
Poland Sp. z o.o., Wrocław